WEARABLE ART FOR KIDS

Clothing Designers and Writers:

Janelle Hayes
Christina Romo Carlisle
Janis Bullis

Publications International, Ltd.

Janelle Hayes owns Kaleidoscope Kids, a home-based design and workshop business that also produces a quarterly newsletter for people who craft with children. She is a member of the Society of Craft Designers.

Christina Romo Carlisle is a craft designer and teacher whose work has appeared in numerous publications, including *Crafts 'N Things, Wearable Wonders,* and *Crochet Fantasy.*

Janis Bullis is a craft designer, writer, and educator who has worked for numerous crafts and fashion magazines, fabric manufacturers, and retailers. She is a member of the Society of Craft Designers, Hobby Industries of America, and Fashion Group International.

Photography: Siede Preis Photography
Production: Brian Warling
Consultant: Janelle Hayes
Hair Stylist: Jay Kemplin
Royal Model Management models: Marvin Charles, Tricia Cook, Blaine Cornelius, Shena Hollingsworth, Kyle Kuhs, Monica Magdziak, Cassady Murphy, Eddie O'Connell, Lauren Rath, Michelle Vergara.

Special thanks to Beth Schwartz, editor, *Wearable Crafts* magazine; Beth Stearns and the Skokie Park District; and The Beadery, whose designs appear on pages 21–26.

The brand-name products mentioned in this publication are service marks or trademarks of their respective companies. The mention of products in directions is merely a record of the procedure used and does not constitute an endorsement by the respective proprietors of Publications International, Ltd., nor does it constitute an endorsement by any of these companies that their products should be used in the manner recommended by this publication.

SOURCES FOR MATERIALS

Materials used on page 7: Duncan Enterprises Scribbles dimensional paint. Materials used on page 10: Duncan Enterprises Scribbles dimensional paint; Therm O Web Heat 'n' Bond Original No Sew fusible webbing. Materials used on page 13: Therm O Web Heat 'n' Bond Original No Sew fusible webbing. Materials used on page 16: Mrs. Grossman's Stickers; Aleene's OK to Wash It fabric glue. Materials used on page 18: Wm. E. Wright Ltd. neon ribbon; Therm O Web Heat 'n' Bond Original No Sew fusible webbing; Dritz Corporation Fray Check seam sealant. Materials used on page 21: The Beadery shoelaces and pony beads. Materials used on page 27: Rubbermaid Contact self-adhesive plastic; Aleene's OK to Wash It fabric glue; Aleene's Ultra Fusible Webbing. Materials used on page 30: The Beadery pony beads; Aleene's Stop Fraying seam sealant. Materials used on page 32: Tulip Crystals Fabric Paint in the Easy-Flow Bottle; Tulip Soft Sparking Tints; Aleene's OK to Wash It fabric glue; Aleen's Transfer It transfer medium. Materials used on page 35: C.M. Offray and Son Inc. ribbon; Dritz Corporation Hem N Trim fusible webbing; Creative Beginnings from the Cotton Ball charms. Materials used on page 38: Karen's Kreations Krinkles gathered ribbon; Aleene's OK to Wash It fabric glue. Materials used on page 41: Tulip Soft Covers All fabric paint; Creative Beginnings from the Cotton Ball charms. Materials used on page 43: Rubbermaid Contact self-adhesive plastic; Delta Starlite fabric dyes; Delta Shiny Stuff fabric paint. Materials used on page 45: Aleene's Ultra Fusible Webbing; Plaid's Fashion Show dimensional paints. Materials used on page 47: Tulip Soft Brush Top fabric paints; Marvy Fabric Marker. Materials used on page 50: Duncan Enterprises Scribbles dimensional paint; Duncan Enterprises Scribbles Brush N Soft fabric paints; Marvy Fabric Marker. Materials used on page 53: Tulip Slick Fine-Line Paint Writer dimensional paints; The Beadery acrylic gemstones. Materials used on page 56: Aleene's Transfer It transfer medium; Aleene's OK to Wash It fabric glue; Therm O Web Heat 'n' Bond Original No Sew fusible webbing; Duncan Enterprises Scribbles dimensional paints; Creative Beginnings from the Cotton Ball charms; The Beadery acrylic gemstones.

CONTENTS

WELCOME TO WEARABLES

As you glance through the projects in *Wearable Art for Kids*, you'll discover wearables for children that are creative, colorful, and contemporary. When choosing projects for this book, there was one rule: Everything must be appropriate for an interested person with enthusiasm but with little experience. The projects are rated "Beginner," "Intermediate," or "Advanced" to give you a further indication of each project's level of involvement. Some are so simple that an adolescent or child could complete them by themselves; others can be done by a child with the help of a supervising adult; and some use detailed techniques that are suitable for adults only.

A few of the projects use more than one technique, but don't be intimidated. Explanations are given in simple, complete, step-by-step instructions. These instructions are accompanied by photographs to make everything easy to understand.

WHAT YOU'LL LEARN

Basic painting involves using a brush or other tool to spread or otherwise manipulate paint or dye on a fabric surface. Begin by pouring a small amount of paint onto a palette, or by dipping your brush into the jar of paint. Brush the paint onto the designated surface in an even fashion. In some cases, you will use a sponge to cover the surface or to fill in a stencil. Some brush-on paints must be heat-set. Read all the labels carefully.

Embellishing refers to applying paint to fabric in order to achieve an embossed effect in which the paint is slightly raised. Most often, this is accomplished by squeezing the paint directly from the bottle onto the fabric and allowing it to dry. Keep the tip of the paint bottle touching the garment in order to fuse the paint directly into the fibers of the fabric.

You may want to practice making lines with the bottle before you try it on your garment. The speed with which you move the bottle will affect the width of the line of paint. Moving quickly will yield a thinner line, while moving slowly will result in a thicker line. Always shake the paint down into the tip of the bottle before you start to squeeze. This helps to remove air bubbles and lessens the chance that the paint will splatter on your work. Wipe the tip frequently with a paper towel to get a clean line.

Sponge-printing refers to applying paint or dye with a shaped sponge. Sponges can be purchased pre-cut, or they can be cut to accommodate any pattern. To make your own shapes, buy a compressed sponge and draw your pattern onto the compressed sponge and cut. Moisten the sponge with water to make it expand. (You can cut shapes from household sponges, but it is very difficult to get sharp, even lines.)

Always moisten your sponges before you paint with them, but be sure to squeeze out the excess water. Too much water in the sponge may cause your design to bleed. The easiest way to paint with a sponge is to pour a puddle of paint onto a palette, dip the sponge in the paint so that the entire surface is covered, and dab off the excess paint onto a clean area of the palette. Gently press the sponge to your garment.

Stencilling involves applying paint inside a template that is then removed to reveal a painted shape. Two methods of stenciling are explained in this book. One method uses freezer paper, which is ironed with the waxy side down onto the garment to be painted. The other method involves clear, self-adhesive shelving paper. Freezer-paper stencils cannot be reused. Stencils made from clear, self-adhesive shelving paper are repositionable and can be reused.

Photo transfer is a technique in which a photograph or postcard can be transferred onto fabric. This technique requires a glue-like product called photo-transfer medium and color photocopies of the photograph or postcard that you choose. Color photocopies can be made at many print shops. If your original photograph has letters or numbers that are visible, be sure to ask for a mirror-image copy. Otherwise, the image will end up reversed. Different photo-transfer mediums have slightly different directions. Read the bottle carefully and follow the manufacturer's instructions.

Applique refers to the attachment of a shape cut from a separate piece of fabric to your garment. In the past, this was accomplished by sewing, but now

you can use an easier method involving iron-on adhesive, also known as fusible webbing. A variety of companies make similar products for different fabric types, ranging from lightweight to extra heavy duty. Be sure to follow the manufacturer's instructions carefully.

WHAT YOU'LL NEED

You won't need all of the products listed here for every project, but you should be aware of the variety of materials that exists. We've made a point of using supplies that a beginner can easily obtain and master. Variety stores, craft shops, art supply stores, and even dime stores carry the equipment listed here.

Paints and dyes. Paints and dyes are made by many companies and are especially formulated for use on fabric. These paints are acrylic based and nontoxic, and you can easily clean up after them with water. Other acrylic paints (such as artists' acrylics) can be used, but they must be mixed with a textile medium to be permanent on fabric.

Dimensional paints come in bottles with an applicator tip. When squeezed directly from the bottle onto the garment, this type of paint will dry with a slightly raised surface. This paint can also be squeezed onto a palette and used with shaped sponges to make prints, or it can be diluted slightly with water and brushed or sponged into a stencil.

Brush-on paints are purchased in jars or bottles. They are generally not as thick as dimensional paints, and they dry with a more flexible texture and a softer look. Some companies make dimensional and brush-on paints in compatible colors.

Fabric dyes are thinner than paint and become a part of the fabric fibers when applied. Dyes are available in dry packages that you mix yourself, or they come premixed in bottles. Some dyes come in a bottle with an applicator tip. Dyes can be squeezed on, brushed on, or sponged on.

Brushes. Only a few specific brushes are used in this book, because only a few are necessary for beginners.

A **sponge brush** consists of a rectangle of fine-grain synthetic sponge angled at the tip. Sponge brushes come in various widths. Most of the projects in this book require a 1-inch-wide sponge brush.

Bristle brushes can be intimidating to the nonpainter because there are so many sizes, widths, and bristle types. Bristles can be made from either natural or synthetic fibers. Synthetic bristles are fine for our purposes, and they're easy to clean. The bristle brushes used most often in this book are shaders, which have chiseled edges that become sharper when wet. These brushes generally give a broad, flat line, but if the edge of the shader is used for applying paint, a fine line results. Round brushes are handy because their bristles come to a point, which allows you to get paint into small areas.

Another type of bristle brush is the stencil brush. It has short, stiff bristles. To use this type of brush, load a small amount of paint onto your brush and dab off excess paint on a paper towel or other surface. Apply the paint inside the stencil by dabbing up and down.

Glues. Use washable fabric glue or industrial-strength adhesive to decorate clothing. Any other type of glue is likely to wash out. If you are working with a child, select a glue that is nontoxic and certified safe for use by children. Another factor to consider is whether the materials you are working with are porous or nonporous. Also, some glues need to be heat-set, while others do not. Read the labels carefully and ask questions of craft store personnel.

For the projects in this book, you will be using glue to attach decorative elements such as gemstones and charms (called embellishments) to your garment. You can also use dimensional paint to attach embellishments.

When using **washable fabric glue** or paint as a glue, squeeze a puddle onto the spot where you want the embellishment, in about the same size and shape. Gently press the item into the puddle. The paint should come up slightly around the edge, but do not press the item all the way down onto the garment. Pressing it all the way to the fabric pushes all the paint or glue out the sides, diminishing the holding power.

On the "Traveler's Denim Jacket," we used an **industrial-strength adhesive.** This glue is toxic and puts out very strong fumes. Follow directions carefully. This is not a glue for children to use, nor should they be around while it is being applied.

Fusible webbing. Iron-on adhesive, or fusible webbing, has a paper backing and is available in several forms. It can be purchased in reels like ribbon; it can be purchased by the yard; or, it can bought in packages of pre-cut sizes. The iron-on adhesive used in this book is double-sided fusible webbing.

Shirt boards. When painting fabric, you must keep it flat, taut, and stable. You also need a surface under the fabric that won't absorb the paint or glue that might soak through. Shirt boards are coated with wax on one side. They can be purchased at craft stores in a variety of sizes.

To use a shirt board, slide the board between the front and back of the garment. Make sure the waxed side is directly under the surface you want to paint. Pull the arms of the garment snugly behind the board, but do not stretch it. Use masking tape to fasten the arms onto the back of the board. Pull the bottom of the shirt up behind the board and fasten it in the same way. It is also possible to make your own shirt board. Get a piece of corrugated cardboard at least 26 by 21 inches in size (for a large adult t-shirt). Trim it to fit snugly inside your garment. Cover one side with waxed paper and use masking tape to secure.

In some cases, you can simply line your shirt or garment with waxed paper rather than using a shirt board. This, however, does not hold your garment as taut and steady as a shirt board.

Pens, pencils, and markers. A variety of pens and markers are used in this book, many of which have specific functions.

Projects that require tracing a pattern or drawing a line of reference onto a garment call for a **disappearing-ink pen** or a **water-soluble pen.** These can be purchased at craft or fabric stores. Water-soluble pens generally use light blue ink that washes out with water. Disappearing-ink pens use ink that is also water-soluble, but it is light purple in color. If you are using either type of pen to trace a pattern onto a garment to be painted, be careful to paint up to the lines, but do not paint over the lines because this encases the line in paint and prevents it from being washed out. Be sure to let

the paint dry thoroughly before trying to remove marker lines.

A few of our projects call for a **dressmaker's pencil** (also called a fabric pencil) to trace a pattern onto dark fabric. These pencils are available most often in blue or white. The white pencils are ideal for marking patterns on black or dark colors. The pencil marks easily wash out or brush off.

Embellishments. You can use almost anything to embellish your garments. Your main considerations need to be washability and safety. Small items that can be pulled off and swallowed by young children should not be used until they are old enough to stop putting things in their mouths.

Acrylic **gemstones** or rhinestones are the most common embellishments. They come in a variety of colors, shapes, and sizes. Any of these can be attached with a washable fabric glue or an industrial-strength adhesive.

We also used **brass charms** to embellish several of our projects. The charms can be sewn on or glued on.

Beads can also be used for wearable art and are available in a variety of sizes, styles, and colors.

Miscellaneous. One of our projects uses a **spin-art machine** to add a specific pattern to fabric patches. Spin-art machines are manufactured by several different companies and can be purchased at toy stores. For a photo and more specific instructions, see the project called "Spooky Spin-Art Spider Webs."

Palettes are used to hold a puddle of paint while you are sponge-painting, stenciling, or brushing on a design. Professional artists' palettes are not necessary. Plastic lids from margarine or whipped topping containers work just as well. You can also use foil, waxed paper, paper plates, or plastic picnic plates.

CHOOSING, PREPARING, AND CARING FOR YOUR GARMENTS

You will get the best results with a fabric that is made from all cotton or a cotton blend. Synthetic fibers simply do not take the paint as well. Always wash and dry a garment before decorating it. Use a laundry detergent without bleach or fabric softeners and do not use fabric softeners.

Never wash a decorated garment until it has set for at least 72 hours. Paint and glue need at least that long to cure, and they will suffer if you wash them too soon.

When a decorated garment is ready to wash, turn it inside out and wash it on a gentle or delicate cycle in warm water. Cold water may cause the paint to crack. Another way to keep the paint soft and flexible is to use liquid fabric softener in the final rinse cycle.

To dry, set the dryer on "Air" and fluff your garment on this setting for a few minutes. If you skipped fabric softener in the wash, use a dryer sheet. After a few minutes in the dryer, remove the garment and let it dry on a line or lay it flat.

YOUR NEW HOBBY

The techniques in *Wearable Art for Kids* can be easily adapted to other designs and types of garments. Also, feel free to work with other colors. Experiment with the Tips and Variations. Thinking about those ideas can lead to a whole new interpretation of a particular project.

Wearables are an expression of your creativity and personality, or your child's personality. The goal is that you will find creating wearable art enjoyable. Happy crafting!

NEON FISH & WAVES

Sponge-print t-shirts are simple to design and easy to produce. This t-shirt and matching visor remind us of a day at the beach or a fabulous vacation. The ocean motifs make the t-shirt a perfect choice to wear over a bathing suit, while the visor will help protect your child from too much sun.

WHAT YOU'LL NEED

- White t-shirt and white plastic visor
- Dimensional fabric paint in bright blue, neon pink, and neon green
- Compressed sponge
- Shirt board
- Yardstick
- Disappearing-ink pen
- Tracing paper, or white paper
- Pencil
- Scissors
- Palette
- Waxed paper

1. Put the t-shirt on a shirt board. To make guidelines for sponge prints, place yardstick across shirt about 2 inches below bottom of neckline. With a disappearing-ink pen, make 2 lines, one above and one below the yardstick. (These lines should be about 1¼ inches apart.) Make 4 more lines each about 1½ inches below the previous one. Then make one last line 1¼ inches (approximate width of yardstick) below those. There should be a total of 7 lines drawn across the shirt front.

2. Trace fish and wave patterns onto white paper or tracing paper and cut out. (Patterns can be found on page 9.) Draw around patterns onto compressed sponge, once for wave and twice for fish. Cut out. Moisten sponges and squeeze out all excess water.

VARIATION

To make a sponge-print shirt even easier, purchase pre-cut sponges. Plan your shirt design around the sponge shapes you find. Pre-cut sponges come in a variety of simple, basic shapes, including stars, anchors, Christmas trees, etc. Your shirt designs can make use of these sponges in either a symmetrical or random fashion. Embellish your sponge-print shirt with glitter paints or acrylic gemstones (embedded into the paint when it is wet).

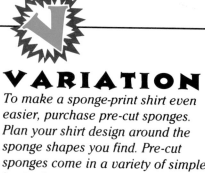

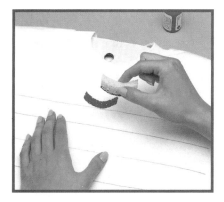  

3. Squirt blue paint onto palette in a puddle about the size of the wave sponge. Dip wave sponge in paint, dab off excess on clean area of palette, and press sponge gently to center of shirt just slightly above the top guideline. Then, working from the center, match edge of sponge with edge of first printed wave to continue row of waves. Make an equal number of waves on each side of first wave. Repeat for second row of waves, aligning each print with the corresponding wave in the row above. Place second row of waves just above the second line.

4. Squirt puddles of neon green and neon pink paint onto palettes. Dip one fish sponge into pink paint, dab off excess, and press to shirt just above the third line, with fish facing left. Using other fish sponge, dip into green paint, dab off excess, and make a green fish print about ⅛ inch to each side of center fish. Green fish should face right. Continue by making pink fish on each side of green ones. Make another row of fish below, starting with the green fish in the center. Make third row of fish identical to first row. Complete shirt by using wave sponge and blue paint to make 2 more rows of waves. (**Note:** On shirt, all pink fish face left and all green fish face right.)

5. To paint the visor, place it on waxed paper. Starting in center and working out, make a row of waves at the top of the visor, curving to conform to shape. Under the waves in the center of the visor, make a green fish facing left. Make pink fish on each side, facing right. Curve around with pink fish to conform to visor shape. Hold visor firmly on waxed paper and make another row of waves below fish, curving completely around visor bill. Run off edge onto waxed paper if necessary. (**Note:** On visor, pink fish face right and green fish face left.)

Neon Fish & Waves
Pattern

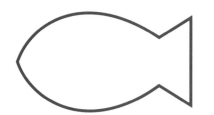

SPOOKY SPIN-ART SPIDER WEBS

Intermediate

Ghosts, ghouls, and goblins galore will be green with envy over this playful Halloween project. Adding to the fun is the imaginative way it is made. In using a spin-art machine, this project will appeal to your children because it utilizes a toy in a new and interesting way. Let them paint the webs and spin the fabric pieces themselves.

WHAT YOU'LL NEED

- Black sweatshirt and black tote bag
- ¼ yard black medium-weight cotton or cotton blend fabric cut into 6 5½×7½-inch pieces
- ½ yard double-sided fusible webbing cut into 6 5×7-inch pieces
- Toy spin-art machine
- Glow-in-the-dark dimensional fabric paint in ghostly glo, pink, green, and yellow
- Shirt board
- Scissors
- Iron and ironing board
- Waxed paper
- Dressmaker's pencil or fabric pencil
- Freezer paper
- Paper towels

1. Following the manufacturer's instructions, fuse rectangles of fusible webbing to fabric rectangles. Trim fabric edges so they are even with edges of fusible webbing. (You might have to adjust rectangle size to fit the size of the card your spin-art machine holds.)

2. Place a fabric rectangle, with fusible webbing already attached, into the card holder of the spin-art machine. Secure all corners. Paint three concentric, irregularly shaped circles about ¾ inch apart on the black fabric with ghostly glo paint. The lines should be about ⅛ inch thick and resemble the circular portion of a spider's web. It is alright for the lines of the outside circle to go off the edges of the fabric.

3. Turn the machine on for about 3 seconds, then turn it off. When fabric stops spinning, the paint should resemble a spider's web. Remove painted fabric patch, set aside to dry, and repeat process for remaining fabric patches. If paint builds up on the outside edge of the machine, use paper towels to wipe it off.

4. When patches are dry, use scissors to trim outside edges into a web shape. Do not cut too close to the outside line of the webs. Cut about ½ inch or so beyond it.

5. Place trimmed patches on shirt and tote bag, overlapping if necessary. Move patches around until you find an arrangement that is pleasing to you. Trace around outside of patches with white fabric pencil.

6. Remove fabric patches, placing each near the area where it will be ironed on. Remove paper backing from first patch, place patch in desired spot using white line as guide, cover with a piece of freezer paper shiny side down, and iron following manufacturer's instructions. Do not iron directly on paint! Let cool and gently peel freezer paper away from patch. Repeat with all patches. If some of the patches overlap, be sure to iron on the bottom patch first.

7. Put shirt on shirt board and line tote bag with waxed paper. Outline patches with ghostly glo paint. Be sure to keep the tip of the bottle on the fabric.

VARIATION

For a pop-art look that is appropriate for any time of the year, try spinning concentric circles in your favorite colors on white fabric. Fuse these to shirts, totebags, and aprons for an item that will be uniquely yours.

8. Use green, pink, and yellow glow-in-the-dark paint to make spiders. These can easily be done freehand. If you feel uncomfortable with that, first practice on a scrap of fabric or a paper towel. To make the spiders, start with a large circle (about the diameter of a quarter) for the body. Fill the circle in with dimensional paint. To make the head, draw and fill in a small circle directly next to the large one. Make four small, upside-down "Vs" on each side of the body to make the spiders' legs. Before making the hanging spider, determine the desired spot. With ghostly glo paint, draw a straight line from inside the web downward until you reach the desired length. Paint a spider, head down, at the bottom of the line.

GONE FISHIN'.

This beginner's project features brightly colored fish designs that were simply cut from fabric and then fused onto a plain, inexpensive white romper. Add the sash to challenge yourself.

Beginner

13

WHAT YOU'LL NEED

- One-piece romper in stretch or woven fabric in light, solid color

- 1-2 yards brightly colored, lightweight, firmly woven print fabric (no knits or stretch material). Fabric should feature large individual motifs with no overlapping.

- Buttons coordinated to match print fabric

- 1-2 yards double-sided fusible webbing

- Pencil

- Scissors

- Tape measure

- Iron and ironing board

Note: Before cutting design motifs from fabric, reserve enough fabric for the sash by cutting two 6×30-inch lengths. Also cut three ½×6-inch lengths and two ½×30-inch lengths of fusible webbing.

1. Cut a motif from the fabric, allowing at least a ½-inch border around the perimeter of the design. Place fusible webbing on table, with the paper side up. Place fabric motif on paper with the right side down. Trace along fabric edge onto paper. Cut fusible webbing ⅛ inch to ¼ inch inside of traced line.

2. Following manufacturer's instructions, fuse webbing to wrong side of fabric motif. Cutting through paper-backed webbing and fabric, cut motif along design lines.

6. Turn under and press 1½ inches along long unfolded edge. Avoid allowing iron to touch any exposed adhesive from the webbing.

 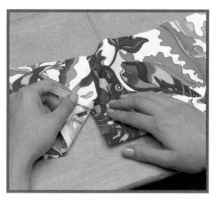 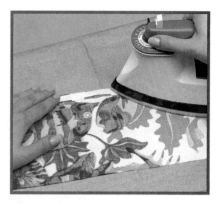

3. Remove paper backing from motif. Position web-backed motif on romper and fuse following manufacturer's instructions. It is suggested that you prepare all motifs with webbing, cut them out, determine their position on the romper, and then fuse them one at a time. Replace romper buttons with coordinating buttons.

4. For the sash, make sure you have reserved two 6×30-inch lengths of fabric. Turn under and press ½ inch on one short end of one length. Following manufacturer's instructions, apply fusible webbing strip to edge that is folded under (seam allowance) and remove paper backing. Fuse to short end of second 6×30-inch fabric length, thereby connecting both lengths of fabric. (**Note:** Do not fold under and press end of second fabric strip. See photo above.)

5. Turn under and press ½ inch on one long edge and on both short ends of seamed sash. Apply fusible webbing to all three folded edges (seam allowances) and then remove paper backing and fuse, following manufacturer's instructions.

7. Lay sash on ironing surface so that long, folded, webbed edge is on top, with adhesive face up. Fold top edge over 1¼ inches, which should overlap cut edge of bottom fold. Press with iron to fuse.

TIP

The matching sash constructed via double-sided fusible webbing turns this project from "Beginner" to "Intermediate." Beginning crafters may want to exclude the matching sash, opting to purchase a belt in a coordinating color.

THE BUGS GO MARCHING 2 BY 2

16

Kids are crazy about stickers. Take advantage of the current craze by incorporating them into this simple wearable-art project. Let your little one get involved by having him or her pick the stickers they want on their shoes.

1. Prepare shoes and cap by washing and drying. (Air dry the cap.) Remove shoelaces from the shoes. Put strip of masking tape around cap where the bill is attached. Arrange stickers on shoes and bill of cap, moving them around until you are satisfied with their placement.

2. Pour a puddle of washable glue onto the palette. Using your finger, spread glue in a thin layer on one shoe at a time. Lift edges of stickers and spread glue under stickers, on bottom of stickers, and on top of stickers. Cover entire bill of cap and canvas surface of shoes with glue. Do *not* put glue onto the tongues of the shoes. The surface of the bill and shoes will have a cloudy appearance while the glue is wet.

3. Let glue dry until it is clear but still tacky. (Drying time varies according to season and temperature.) Use sponge brush to apply a thin, even coat of glue over entire area. Press down any sticker edges that pop up. If small bubbles appear when you are applying glue, brush until they disappear because the bubbles will not dry clear. Repeat drying time and apply a third coat of glue with the sponge brush. The shoes need at least three coats of glue, while the cap can get by with two. Let shoes and cap dry thoroughly before wearing.

VARIATION

The wide variety of stickers available makes this project easily adaptable to any occasion or holiday. Try Easter egg stickers on pastel-colored shoes for the neighborhood egg hunt, or use American flag stickers on white shoes for the Fourth of July parade.

RIBBON ROUNDUP

Kids love to use buttons, pins, decorative fabric, or other materials to make their denim jackets unique expressions of their individuality. Help your teens express themselves with this bold use of colored ribbon.

Advanced

WHAT YOU'LL NEED

- Denim jeans and jacket
- 6 different colors each of ⅜-inch and ⅝-inch-wide neon-colored satin ribbon. To determine quantity of ribbon needed, estimate 1½ yards per 3 running inches along leg, jacket front, and jacket yoke.
- Double-sided fusible webbing, 17 inches wide by length of jeans leg. This should allow enough for both jeans and jacket.
- 10-15 yards ½-inch-wide double-sided fusible webbing for seam allowances
- Tracing paper
- Straight pins
- Pencil
- Ruler
- Scissors
- Water-soluble pen
- Iron and ironing board
- Seam sealant (optional)
- Fabric glue (optional)

TIP

A great deal of ribbon is needed to complete both the jeans and jacket. Consider doing only the jeans or the jacket, which should cut your ribbon usage by about half.

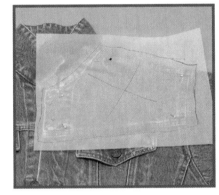

1. Pin a piece of tracing paper on the jacket or jeans and trace the general shape of the area to be covered with ribbon, allowing about a ½-inch overlap on all sides. Draw diagonal lines at right angles to each other in the direction you want the ribbons to follow. This mark will serve as your starting point for placing the ribbons.

2. Remove tracing from jacket, and straighten the drawn edges with a ruler. Trace this shape onto a sheet of fusible webbing and cut. Cut 2 of this shape, one a mirror image of the other. Follow the shape of the jacket for the yoke shape. The vertical strips on the front of the jacket we used measure 3½×13 inches; the pants leg strips measure 3½×36 inches. (Our jacket and pants are a girl's size 14.) On the adhesive side of pattern, using a water soluble pen, carefully—without ripping the adhesive—draw a cross at right angles to each other in the direction you want the ribbons to run, just as in Step 1.

3. Place fusible webbing pattern on ironing board, adhesive side up. Selecting colors and widths at random, cut several pieces of ribbon long enough to cover length of pattern. Begin placement of ribbons on pattern at marked cross, working your way to the ends. Using straight pins, pin ribbons to ironing board as you cover pattern. Continue to cut ribbons in random colors and widths and pin to board until pattern is covered. Ribbons for yoke pattern will be varying lengths. Ours were cut 4 to 6 inches long. Ribbons for vertical strips on jacket and pants will all be the same length. Ours were cut 6 inches long.

 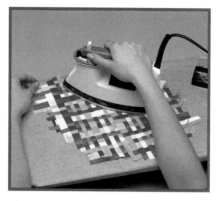 

4. Cut a few ribbons to cover length of pattern in opposite direction. Because the pattern is covered with ribbons at this point, refer to marked cross on tracing paper to position ribbons correctly. Beginning at center, weave a ribbon under and over each pinned ribbon. Keep all ribbons flat and at right angles. Also make sure they cover entire pattern.

5. When all vertical and horizontal ribbons are woven in place, fuse ribbon to webbing, carefully removing pins as you press. Caution: Follow manufacturer's instructions for fusing. Do not allow temperature of iron to exceed suitable temperature for ribbons. Be especially cautious when using silk, lightweight, or finely printed ribbon. Too high of a temperature can cause too much adhesive to bond to ribbons. Once fused, turn ribbon assembly over and press again on paper side to secure fusing. Cut off all ribbon tails along edge of paper then remove paper backing.

6. With right side facing up, place ribbon fabric over area of denim to be covered. (For the jacket yoke, place appropriate ribbon fabric over yoke, mark where the button hole should be, and cut a slit in the ribbon fabric for the button hole. If desired, use seam sealant to stop fraying where ribbon fabric was slit. Return ribbon fabric to yoke.) Turn under and pin ½-inch seam allowance on all edges, but do not pin ribbon fabric to denim.

7. Remove ribbon fabric from denim. With wrong side of ribbon fabric facing up, fuse webbing strips to all edges of seam allowances. Fuse only seam allowances, do not allow iron to touch center fused area of ribbon fabric. Remove paper backing.

8. Return ribbon fabric to denim and iron over entire area, fusing ribbon fabric to area. Repeat for all ribbon fabric pieces. A little dab of fabric glue will help to hold trouble spots.

RAINBOW LOOPS & BEADS

Neon-colored pony beads make a striking decoration for any wearable-art project. The shoes and sweatshirt that make up this combination can be worn separately or as a matching set.

21

WHAT YOU'LL NEED

Shoes

- 1 pair high-top gym shoes
- 1 pair neon pink shoelaces
- 12×10mm neon heart-shaped pony beads: 6 orange, 6 green, 6 yellow, 2 blue
- 9×6mm neon barrel-shaped pony beads: 2 orange, 2 green, 2 yellow, 2 blue
- 12mm opaque sunburst beads: 2 orange, 4 yellow, 6 baby blue, 4 pink

- 6mm opaque round beads: 6 yellow, 6 baby blue, 4 pink, 2 orange
- 6 snowman-face beads, 14mm each
- 10 silver jump rings, 8mm each
- 10 silver head pins, 1½-inch each
- Long-nose pliers
- Round-nose pliers

1. String beads onto head pins by following the charts below for the correct order of the various bead configurations, then follow the diagram titled "Making a Head Pin Loop" to complete tops of bead configurations. Use wire cutters to trim the pin if necessary, then use round-nose pliers to bend the end of the pin into a small loop, stringing on a jump ring (see above). Repeat for a total of 4 heart-bead configurations and 6 snowman-face configurations.

Snowman-Face Configurations

Note: Make one of each color for each shoe. Work from the bottom of the head pin up.

1 12mm opaque yellow sunburst bead
1 14mm snowman-face bead
1 12mm opaque orange sunburst bead
1 6mm opaque baby blue round bead

1 12mm opaque baby blue sunburst bead
1 14mm snowman-face bead
1 12mm opaque pink sunburst bead
1 6mm opaque yellow round bead

1 12mm opaque pink sunburst bead
1 14mm snowman-face bead
1 12mm opaque yellow sunburst bead
1 6mm opaque orange round bead

Making A Head Pin Loop

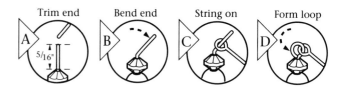

Trim end · Bend end · String on · Form loop

A 5/16" B C D

Heart-bead Configurations Chart

Note: Make 2 of these for each shoe. Work from the bottom of the head pin up.

1 6mm opaque pink round bead
1 12mm opaque baby blue sunburst bead
1 6mm opaque yellow round bead
1 12×10mm neon orange heart-shaped pony bead
1 6mm opaque baby blue round bead

  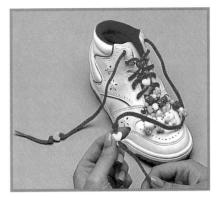

2. String 4 barrel beads, 2 heart-bead configurations, and 3 snow-man-face configurations onto one of the shoelaces in the order shown in photo. Center these items on the shoelace and string lace ends from front to back through bottom eyelets of shoe.

3. String a neon green heart-shaped pony bead (small end first) onto ends of both shoelaces held together (see above). Bring each lace up through the next eyelet on each side of the shoe. String a neon yellow heart-shaped pony bead onto ends of both shoelaces held together. Bring each lace down through the next eyelet on each side of the shoe. String a neon orange heart-shaped pony bead onto both lace ends held together. Bring each lace end down through the next eyelet on each side of the shoe. String a neon blue heart-shaped pony bead onto both lace ends held together. Bring each lace end down through the next eyelet on each side of the shoe. String a neon green heart-shaped pony bead onto both lace ends held together. Bring each lace end down through the next eyelet on each side of the shoe. Finally, string a neon yellow heart-shaped pony bead onto both lace ends held together. Bring each lace end up through the top eyelet on each side of the shoe. (**Note:** More or fewer eyelets on the shoe will require more or fewer heart-shaped pony beads.)

4. Tie a single knot about 3 inches from one end of the shoelace. String on a neon yellow heart-shaped pony bead. Tie another knot to hold the bead. Repeat with the other end, using a neon green heart-shaped pony bead. Repeat Steps 2–4 to make a second shoelace.

WHAT YOU'LL NEED

Sweatshirt

- 1 white sweatshirt
- 9×6mm barrel-shaped pony beads: 30 magenta, 58 neon yellow, 53 neon blue, 58 neon orange, 56 neon green
- 53-inch neon shoelaces: 10 green, 10 pink, 1 yellow, 3 blue
- Scissors
- Ruler
- Fabric glue, or needle & and thread
- Straight pins

Note: The shoelaces pictured are a round style, made of loosely woven poly-propylene. If similar laces are not available, you may use regular shoe-laces, sewing the loops with a heavy thread and large needle instead. Very tightly woven laces may not be suitable. The sweatshirt pictured is size 7-8. The number of shoelaces and beads used may be varied to suit the size of the sweatshirt.

VARIATION

Use your imagination to develop your own color combinations for Rainbow Loops & Beads. Try substituting pastel versions of the colors on the charts for a springtime look, or autumnal colors for the fall.

1. Trim the tip of the plastic end of a blue lace at a sharp angle, making a point. You will use this pointed lace as the "needle and thread."

2. Measure 3 inches from one end of a green lace. Thread the blue lace through the middle of the green lace.

3. Measure another ½ inch on the green lace and thread the blue lace through the middle of the green lace once again, as shown. String a magenta barrel bead onto the green lace.

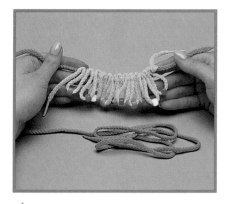  

4. Measure 3 more inches on the green lace and thread the blue lace through it. Measure another ½ inch and thread the blue lace through the green lace once again. Repeat Steps 2–3 until 3 inches of the green shoelace are left (12 loops with beads). Alternate the colors of the beads, repeating the following order: magenta, yellow, blue, and orange. After the last 3-inch loop, measure and thread on 1 more ½-inch loop, with no bead.

5. Repeat Steps 2–4 to add more green laces. A total of 8 green laces will make a row of loops around the yoke of a child's size 7-8 sweatshirt. Work the loops down along the blue lace as you complete each green lace.

6. Repeat Steps 1–5 to make the row of pink loops, substituting the neon pink shoelaces for the green ones and using a second blue lace as the needle and thread. Alternate blue, orange, green, and yellow beads.

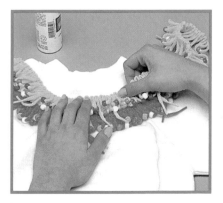

7. Pin the pink row of loops in an oval shape approximately 2½ inches below the neck seam. Gather and adjust the loops to fit the oval shape of the yoke. Glue or sew the row of loops to the sweatshirt all the way around the front and back. The line of glue or sewing should be along the blue lace, allowing the longer loops to hang freely to form a fringe. Trim the ends of the blue lace to ¼ inch. Tuck them in and securely glue or sew them under so they don't show. Measure ¾ inch up from the pink row of loops and attach the green row of loops in the same way. (The green loops will hang down to cover the top edge of the pink row of loops.)

Flower Chart

Step 8 Flower			Step 9 Flower		Step 10 Knot
Needle & Thread	Petals	Beads	Needle & Thread	Petals	
green	pink	yellow, green, orange, blue	pink	green	pink
yellow	green	magenta, orange, blue, yellow	green	yellow	green
pink	yellow	orange, blue, green, magenta	pink	pink	yellow
green	blue	orange, magenta, green, lemon	green	green	blue

8. Using a green lace as the needle and thread, make 5 loops of pink lace with yellow, blue, orange, and green beads as shown. Loops should measure 1¾ inches. Push the loops together and tie the green lace used as the needle and thread in a single knot. Trim all 4 ends to ½ inch. Glue the ends to the middle of the flower.

9. Make a smaller flower from a green lace but without beads. Loops should measure 1 inch. Glue or sew to the center of the flower with beads made in Step 8.

10. Cut a 4-inch length of pink lace. Tie a double knot. Trim both ends to ½ inch and glue or sew against the knot. Glue or sew the knot to the center of the Step 9 flower.

11. Repeat Steps 8–10 to make 4 more flowers in different colors. See chart above for color suggestions. Glue flowers to front of sweatshirt. We used 2 flowers with the pink and green combination, and 1 each of the others.

12. Glue or sew 8 beads evenly spaced along the cuff of each sleeve, alternating colors in orange, magenta, yellow, and green.

SPRINGTIME SHADOW APPLIQUE

Many wearable-art projects emphasize primary colors, but this delicate design features the soft pastels of silk flowers.

Intermediate

WHAT YOU'LL NEED

- White t-shirt
- 2 or 3 bunches of silk flowers in at least 2 different sizes and colors (we used large pink mums and small purple violets)
- 1 bunch of silk ivy leaves
- ½ yard organza, or chiffon
- Approximately 100 pearls, 3mm each
- 15-20 crystal E beads
- 4 acrylic stars, 15mm each
- 2 yards ½-inch-wide lace with bound edge
- Tracing paper, or clear self-adhesive shelving paper
- Double-sided fusible webbing
- 2 pressing cloths
- Measuring tape
- Pencil
- Scissors
- Shirt board
- Washable fabric glue
- Straight pins

1. Lay t-shirt on flat surface. Pull shoulder seams slightly forward so they are visible at front of shirt. Smooth the rest of shirt out into its true shape. Cut a piece of tissue paper or clear shelving paper large enough to cover front of t-shirt from approximately armhole to armhole and from top of shoulder to below armholes. Lay tissue paper over top of shirt and pin in place. If you are using clear shelving paper, remove paper backing and adhere sticky side to top of shirt. Determine top of yoke pattern by tracing around neckline about 1 inch below neck ribbing. Measure shoulder seam to determine width of yoke pattern. The length of the shoulder seam is the width of the yoke pattern. Measure and mark that distance in regular increments as you move measuring tape around the neck (measure from the line that you marked off for the top of the yoke pattern). Complete pattern by tracing shoulder seams. (See photo for clarity.) If you are using tissue paper, mark an X on right side of the pattern.

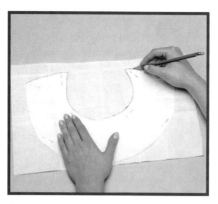

2. Remove tissue or shelving paper pattern from shirt and cut out yoke along outline. Pin pattern wrong side up on paper backing of fusible webbing and trace yoke pattern. If using shelving paper, stick pattern to adhesive side of web; then trace. Remove pattern and cut yoke out of adhesive web along outline.

3. Place fusible webbing, adhesive side down, on t-shirt. Adjust and smooth out t-shirt so webbing covers entire yoke area below neck ribbing. Following manufacturer's instructions, bond webbing to t-shirt. Remove paper backing.

7. Slip t-shirt over shirt board. Working on a single flower at a time, squeeze a small circle of fabric glue on center of a larger flower. Drop about 15-20 pearls into glue, using a toothpick to roll them into place. The size of glue circle and number of pearls needed will vary with each flower. On smallest flowers, place a drop of glue in center of each and place 3 crystal E beads in glue. Arrange acrylic stars on t-shirt. Carefully lifting each star from shirt, use toothpick to coat back of stars with fabric glue. Glue stars in place on garment. Allow glue to dry.

8. Cut lace long enough to fit along bottom edge of yoke from shoulder to shoulder. At right shoulder, squeeze a 3-inch line of glue along bottom edge of organza. With ruffles pointing down, press bound edge of lace into glue. Pin in place every inch, inserting pin through lace, t-shirt, and into shirt board. Repeat gluing along bottom of yoke. Cut lace long enough to fit along top edge of yoke and repeat; gluing lace just below ribbing. Cut 2 pieces of lace to fit over each shoulder seam. Glue to shirt at each shoulder.

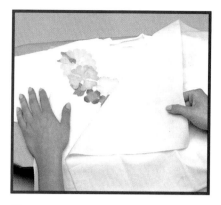

4. Pin or stick pattern right side up on organza and cut yoke out. Leave pattern attached to organza yoke until you are ready to use it to identify the right side of the yoke. Set aside.

5. Remove silk flowers and leaves from stems. Separate layers of flowers. Some flowers may require wire cutters to remove center. Discard any plastic parts of flowers, including centers. Press flowers and leaves slightly to flatten. Arrange flowers and leaves over webbing, overlapping as desired. When satisfied with arrangement, tack in place by pressing the point of a hot iron to each flower and leaf for a second or two.

6. Remove yoke pattern from organza yoke and place organza yoke right side up over floral arrangement, covering all of the webbing. Cover yoke area with pressing cloth. Following manufacturer's instructions, bond floral arrangment under organza to t-shirt. Pressing cloth may stick to organza slightly, but can be removed with a gentle pull.

TIP

Test flowers and leaves for color fastness by soaking them in water and gentle soap for a few minutes. Agitate gently in soapy water. Check water for excessive dye. Rinse flowers and leaves and place on paper towel to dry.

JINGLE BELLS

Jingle Bells is a simple holiday project that most school-age children can do by themselves. With a minimum of materials and just a small investment of time, your kids will be sporting a colorful, festive look. Also, the bells will let you know if they are sneaking into the Christmas packages ahead of time!

WHAT YOU'LL NEED

- 1 pair white tennis shoes
- 2¾ yards ⅜-inch-wide red grosgrain ribbon cut into 4 lengths at 12 inches each, and 2 lengths at 25½ inches each
- 4 jingle bells, 18mm each
- 67 green barrel-shaped pony beads
- 1½ yards gold elastic cord cut into 3 lengths at 8 inches each, and 1 length at 30 inches
- Scissors
- Anti-fraying glue

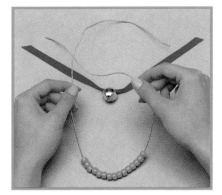

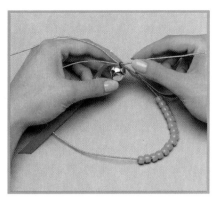

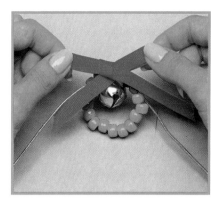

1. For the necklace, thread 12 inches of red ribbon through jingle bell until bell is centered on ribbon. String 15 pony beads on 30 inches of elastic cord. Hold ends of cord up so beads fall to center. Lay bell and cord flat on table with bell centered above cord.

2. Thread right end of elastic cord from right to left through jingle bell. Thread left end of elastic cord from left to right through jingle bell. Pull each end through so bell is centered in a circle of pony beads. Knot gold cord at top of jingle bell.

3. Tie the red ribbon into a bow. Trim the ends diagonally and apply anti-fraying glue to edges. Tie the ends of the gold cord in a square knot. Trim the ends and apply anti-fraying glue.

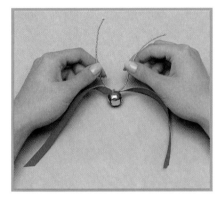

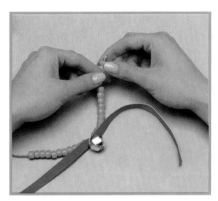

4. To make a bracelet, thread 12 inches of red ribbon and 8 inches of gold cord through the jingle bell, centering each.

5. Thread 11 pony beads onto each side of the jingle bell on the gold cord. Pull the ends of the gold cord and tie in a square knot. Trim the ends and apply anti-fraying glue. Hide the knot inside the beads. Tie the ribbon into a bow. Trim the ends diagonally and apply anti-fraying glue to the cut edges.

6. For each shoelace, use a 25½-inch length of ribbon. Cut each end diagonally and apply anti-fraying glue to the cut edges. Repeat Steps 1 and 2 completely, except string the beads on 8 inches of elastic cord. After knotting the cord at the top of the jingle bell, tie cord around center of the ribbon shoelace. Tie the 12-inch length of ribbon into a bow, trim ends diagonally, and apply anti-fraying glue.

7. Lace shoes with jingle bell wreaths in center.

TIP

For very small children, adjust the length of the cord for the necklace so that the beaded bell does not fall below the middle of the abdomen.

MAKING A SPLASH!

Advanced

If your son or daughter excels at a particular sport, this is a great way to display their team spirit. With this project, you can transfer the team's best photo to your child's favorite t-shirt so they can show off their winning team with pride.

WHAT YOU'LL NEED

- White t-shirt
- Color photocopy of desired photograph. (If there are numbers or letters in your photograph, be sure to ask for a mirror-image copy at the print shop!)
- Photo-transfer medium
- Blue crystal dimensional fabric paint
- Aqua or blue soft sparkling fabric paint
- Fabric paint brushes (we used a flat shader and a medium round)
- 1-inch sponge brush
- Palette
- Scissors
- Waxed paper
- Rolling pin
- Iron and ironing board
- Pressing cloth
- Washable fabric glue
- White paper
- Black marker
- Disappearing-ink pen
- Shirt board

1. Place your shirt on a shirt board. If your shirt board has dried paint on it, cover it with waxed paper, because dried paint may transfer to the inside of your shirt and discolor your photo. Trim all white edges from photocopy. Lay photocopy face up on waxed paper. Apply a thick layer of transfer medium with finger or sponge brush. Be sure all edges and corners have been covered.

2. Place photocopy face down on center of shirt, about 3½ inches from base of neckline. Smooth onto shirt with rolling pin, making sure to remove any air bubbles. If any transfer medium is pressed out of the sides, wipe it up immediately. Dry flat for 24 hours.

VARIATION

The splash design works well with a swimming picture and blue paint, but you can also use the same pattern with any team photo for any sport. Simply change the paint to the colors of your team or other colors that will coordinate with your photo, and you can make a splash even if you're not a swimmer!

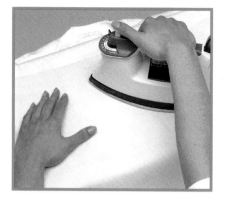

3. After 24 hours, remove shirt from shirt board and heat-set both sides of transfer for 30 seconds using a pressing cloth and a dry iron on a wool setting. Let cool.

4. Soak shirt in water for 30 to 60 minutes. Remove from water. Squeeze excess water from shirt, but do not wring transfer area. Lay shirt on a clean, flat surface. Using your fingers, gently rub paper backing. Work from the center of the transfer to the outside edges. When you have removed the first layer of paper, return shirt to water to soak for another 15 minutes. Remove from water, repeating process until all paper particles have been removed. Be especially careful when rubbing edges so as not to tear the transfer. Let shirt dry flat. (Transfer may appear cloudy.)

5. When all paper particles have been removed and shirt is dry, return shirt to shirt board. Pour a puddle of washable glue onto palette and use sponge brush to apply a thin coat to the transfer area. Set aside to dry.

6. Trace splash patterns onto separate sheets of white paper with black marker. (Patterns can be found on page 60.) Place patterns inside shirt above and to right of transfer, aligning corners of splash with corner of photo. Trace patterns onto shirt with disappearing-ink pen. Repeat, moving patterns below and to left of transfer.

7. Use fabric paint brushes to brush soft sparkling fabric paint inside of splash lines. Squeeze blue crystal paint from bottle in a line around the edge of the transfer. Use the flat shader brush to flatten line of paint in a wavy fashion.

TUXEDO
JUNCTION

Dress up a plain tuxedo shirt with colorful ribbons and decorative charms. Your teenager will love the casual elegance that makes this project a popular one. Ask your favorite teen to help you by selecting and cutting the necessary ribbons.

Advanced

WHAT YOU'LL NEED

- ✗ Tuxedo shirt
- ✗ 7-9 ⅝-inch-wide buttons, or sized to fit button holes
- ✗ 1½ yards ⅜-inch-wide polka dot grosgrain ribbon, or 2× length of pleats + 4 inches
- ✗ 1½ yards ⅜-inch-wide picot edge satin, or 2× length of pleats + 4 inches
- ✗ 1½ yards ⅝-inch-wide grosgrain, or 2× length of pleats + 4 inches
- ✗ 1½ yards medium rickrack, or 2× length of pleats + 4 inches
- ✗ 3 yards ⅜-inch-wide striped satin ribbon, or 2× length of pleats + 2× length of cuffs + 2× length of sleeve plackets + 12 inches for clean finished edges and mitered corners

- ✗ 4 yards 1-inch-wide printed grosgrain ribbon, or 2× length of pleats + width of pleats + 2× length of cuffs + length of collar + 16 inches for clean finished edges and mitered corners
- ✗ Double-sided fusible webbing equal in length and width, or slightly narrower, to ribbon (we chose 1 package each of ¼-inch, ½-inch, and ¾-inch widths)
- ✗ 10 ⅜-inch to ¾-inch brass charms in assorted shapes (we chose hearts, stars and keys)
- ✗ Needle and thread
- ✗ Iron and ironing board
- ✗ 10-15 straight pins

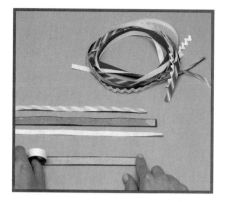

1. Remove decorative studs and buttons from shirt front. Cut 2 lengths of 26 inches each from polka dot, picot edge, ⅝-inch grosgrain, and striped ribbons, or length of pleated front plus 2 inches. Following manufacturer's instructions, apply fusible webbing to wrong side of 8 lengths of ribbon. Cut 2 lengths of 26 inches each, or length of pleated front plus 2 inches, from rickrack.

TIP

Though rickrack can be fused onto ribbon in Step 2, sewing it on with a sewing machine provides a neater and more secure bond.

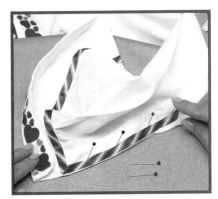

2. With webbed side facing down, position ribbon on pleated front. Begin with striped ribbon nearest center, continue toward outer edge with picot-edge satin ribbon, polka dot ribbon, and then ⅝-inch grosgrain nearest outer edge of pleats. Turn under ½ inch at top edge and line up evenly with seam of shirt. Allow ribbon to extend only ½ inch past pleated edge at bottom. Trim ribbon if necessary. Using straight pins, pin ribbon through shirt, directly to ironing board. Following manufacturer's instructions, press ribbon and fuse onto shirt. Sew or fuse rickrack to center of ⅝-inch grosgrain.

3. Cut 2 lengths of 1-inch-wide printed ribbon, each 33 inches long, or length of pleated front plus ½ width of pleated front plus 4 inches. Following manufacturer's instructions, apply fusible webbing to wrong side of each length of ribbon. With webbed side facing down, position ribbon on shirt, outside of pleated front on flat part of shirt. Begin by turning under ½ inch at top edge and lining up fold with shoulder seam. Position along side edge and miter ribbon at corner; then position along bottom edge, covering cut ends of narrower ribbons as shown. Turn under ½ inch of ribbon at the edge of the shirt placket, lining up fold with placket. Using straight pins, pin ribbon through shirt directly to ironing board. Following manufacturer's instructions, press ribbon and fuse onto shirt.

4. Fold cuffs up (almost in half) just below the buttonhole and along the entire length, and press. Stitch along fold if desired. Cut 2 lengths of wide printed ribbon equal to length of cuff plus 1 inch. Apply fusible webbing to wrong side of ribbon. Position ribbon for outside of cuff along folded edge. Turn under ends for clean finish. Fuse into place. Stitch along all edges if desired. Cut 2 lengths of striped ribbon equal to length of cuff plus length of sleeve placket plus 3 inches. Apply fusible webbing to wrong side of ribbon. Turn under one end for clean finish. Position ribbon to outside of cuff at top edge, miter at corner and position along placket. Turn under remaining edge. Fuse into place. Stitch along all edges if desired.

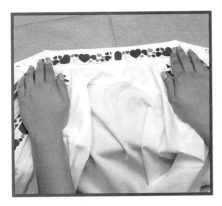

5. Cut length of printed ribbon equal to length of collar plus 1 inch. Apply fusible webbing to wrong side of ribbon. Center ribbon to outside of collar as shown. Turn under each end to clean finish. You may need to fold at an angle to follow bend in the collar. Fuse into place. Stitch along all edges if desired.

6. Randomly stitch charms into place on satin ribbon and collar points. Replace shirt buttons with decorative buttons at shirt front.

BO PEEP'S SHEEP

You'll think that Bo Peep just stepped off the pages of a story book when your little girl steps into these colorful overalls.

- Toddler's bib overalls
- 6 inches pink crinkled ribbon
- 6 inches yellow crinkled ribbon
- 9 inches light blue crinkled ribbon
- 1 yard white crinkled ribbon
- 18 inches ⅛-inch-wide double-faced chartreuse satin ribbon
- ⅜-inch-diameter black shank button
- Scrap of black felt
- Scrap of white felt
- Large safety pin
- Washable fabric glue
- Scissors
- Toothpicks
- Straight pins
- Tracing paper
- Pencil
- White fabric or dressmaker's pencil
- Needle and white thread, or glue gun
- Corrugated cardboard covered with waxed paper (optional)

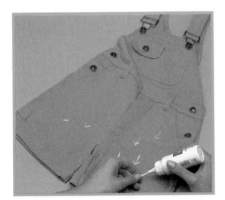

1. Beginners are advised to slip garment over covered cardboard, though the cardboard is not visible in this photo. Cut chartreuse satin ribbon on a slant into 7 lengths at ¾-inch each for stems and 18 lengths at ½-inch each for leaves. Stems are placed vertically onto garment with 2 leaves angled in a V-shape at the bottom of each stem. Arrange 5 stems with accompanying leaves on right leg and 2 stems with leaves on bib as shown in photo on page 38. Arrange 4 remaining leaves into 2 Vs to make blades of grass on left leg. Dip toothpick into fabric glue to coat backs of stems and leaves, beginning with those at bottom of garment and working your way to the top.

2. Cut pink, blue, and yellow crinkled ribbon into 3-inch lengths, 2 for each color. To form a flower, bend one end of crinkled ribbon down about ¼ inch and tightly roll the rest of ribbon around this end. To hold ribbon in roll shape, insert straight pin into outside end of ribbon and through the roll, coming out through the opposite side of roll. Repeat this step with each of the remaining 3-inch ribbon lengths.

3. Completely cover one side of rolled ribbon with fabric glue. Glue rolled-ribbon flower to top of a stem on garment, holding in place with 2 straight pins stuck through the flower, through the garment, and into cardboard (if using it). Do not remove pins until glue has completely dried. Glue remaining rolled-ribbon flowers to garment on green ribbon stems.

4. To make sheep, roll up entire piece of white crinkled ribbon as described in Step 3. Stick several pins through roll to hold it together. Cut a circle of white felt slightly smaller than the size of rolled ribbon (about 2½ inches in diameter). Completely cover one side of rolled ribbon with fabric glue. Place felt circle over glue side of rolled ribbon. Set aside to dry.

5. Draw sheep's ear and leg shapes freehand onto tracing paper and cut out. Using these as a pattern, trace ears and legs onto black felt with white fabric pencil and cut out. When the white rolled ribbon representing the sheep's body is completely dry, flip over with felt side down on table. Position ears in center of sheep's body and position legs under bottom edge of body, as pictured. Place button below ears for sheep's face. Spread fabric glue evenly over back of ears and glue on body of sheep. Squeeze a small circle of fabric glue below ears. Place shank of button into glue. Allow to dry. Spread glue on top of legs and affix them to felt side of sheep's body near the bottom.

6. Attach safety pin to back of sheep either by sewing into place with white thread or by gluing with hot glue. Attach sheep button to bibs on left leg as shown. The safety pin allows you to detach the sheep button for laundering.

VARIATION

Create this design on different types of garments. Consider making a coordinated outfit featuring a cotton knit skirt and top decorated in crinkled-ribbon flowers, with the sheep grazing on the crown of a matching sun hat. For each additional flower, increase satin ribbon length by 1½ inches and crinkled ribbon by 3 inches.

With the delicate look of these heart and key charms, this project is sure to catch the fancy of your teenager. What a great mother-daughter project!

Intermediate

KEYS TO MY HEART

- Dark-colored t-shirt
- Brass charms in key and heart shapes (other charms can be substituted)
- Fabric paint in pink, teal, and purple
- Fabric paint brushes (we used a flat shader)
- Tracing paper
- Pencil
- 11×9-inch piece of tulle
- Black marker
- Shirt board
- Masking tape
- White fabric or dressmaker's pencil
- Iron and ironing board
- Needle and thread to match shirt color

VARIATION

Brass charms are available in a wide variety of styles and sizes. Try a nautical theme by using sailboat, anchor, and flag charms on a white shirt painted with red, blue, and yellow design elements. Or, try a western theme by using charms shaped like cacti, cowboy boots, and horses on a brown shirt painted in turquoise, coral, and cream.

1. Prepare shirt by washing and drying. Lay charms you have chosen onto pattern in book to determine whether or not you need to adjust pattern. (Pattern can be found on page 61.) Charms should be placed in empty spaces between design elements. Trace pattern onto tracing paper, making changes if necessary. Tape tulle onto traced pattern and mark over lines with black marker.

2. Put shirt on shirt board. Position tulle pattern on shirt in desired spot and tape in place. Trace over lines with fabric or dressmaker's pencil. Remove tulle.

3. To paint, start at top of shirt and work your way down. Rows with rectangles are painted pink, rows with thin waves are teal, and rows with thick waves are purple. On a very dark-colored shirt, you may need to apply a second coat of paint.

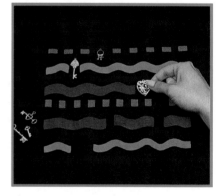

4. When shirt is completely dry, heat-set paint following manufacturer's instructions. Place charms in desired spots and sew.

FUN ON THE BEACH

Your son can hang ten or just hang out in this colorful action-wear, which is perfect for the pool or beach!

WHAT YOU'LL NEED

- T-shirt and pair of shorts
- Soft fabric paints in 5 colors (we used brown, white, gold, red, and orange)
- Shiny dimensional fabric paint (we used red)
- ½-inch stencil brush
- Small round brush
- Pencil
- Clear self-adhesive shelving paper
- Small sharp scissors
- Shirt board
- Palettes
- Paper towels
- Cardboard
- Waxed paper or plastic wrap

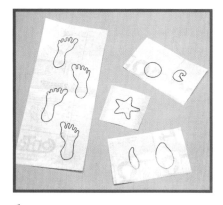

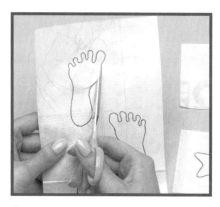

1. Place t-shirt over shirt board. Cut a piece of cardboard large enough to fit through the leg of the shorts. Cover one side with waxed paper or plastic wrap. Place cardboard through one leg of shorts with front of shorts over covered side. Cut shelving paper into a 5×11-inch rectangle, 2 3½×5½-inch rectangles, and a 3-inch square. Placing shelving paper over patterns, trace outlines of footprint pattern onto 5×11-inch rectangle; trace Shell Pattern No. 1 on one 3½×5⅓-inch rectangle and Shell Pattern No. 2 on the other 3½×5⅓-inch rectangle; trace starfish pattern on the 3-inch square. (Patterns can be found on page 62.)

2. Cut out all stencils as follows: With point of a small pair of scissors, punch a hole through center of your patterns. Cut out each pattern, carefully following the outlines. Do not cut outside of the outlines.

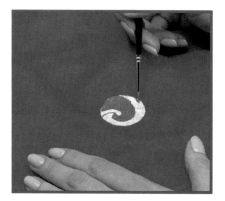

5. Applying paint directly from bottle, paint red dots with shiny dimensional paint over starfish as indicated on pattern. With brown fabric dye or soft paint and No. 00 round brush, draw in lines on Shell No. 2 as shown. Allow paints to dry completely.

TIP

Self-adhesive plastic is a great substitute for heavy stencil paper or mylar, which are usually used for stencils. You can easily trace the design through the paper backing, and you can cut the thin plastic with a small pair of craft scissors instead of a matte knife. With its sticky back, stencils cut from self-adhesive plastic hold tightly to the shirt without using toxic adhesive sprays.

3. Remove paper backing from footprint stencil. Place along left front side of shirt as pictured, rubbing firmly over entire stencil to ensure that all edges are tightly stuck to shirt. Pour a small amount of brown fabric dye or soft paint onto palette. Dip stencil brush into paint and tap 2 or 3 times on palette to remove excess paint. Firmly tap brush over open area of stencil until brush is dry. Dip brush into paint again, tap off excess on palette and resume painting across stencil. Once all footprints have been stenciled onto shirt, carefully lift off stencil and wipe clean of paint with damp paper towel. Affix stencil to front of right leg of shorts. Following stencil instructions above, stencil footprint design onto shorts with gold paint. Stencil Part A of Shell No. 1 onto right shoulder of t-shirt with brown paint by repeating stenciling procedure; with orange, stencil starfish onto lower left corner of shirt; with white, stencil Part A of Shell No. 2 onto front of lower left leg of shorts.

4. When paints are completely dry (at least 1 hour), paint Part B of each shell over corresponding Part A. Place Part B stencil over already-painted Part A for each shell. Stencil as described in Step 3, painting Part B of Shell No. 1 with red and Part B of Shell No. 2 with brown.

Your little copilot can pretend to fly high in the sky in this charming sweatshirt, suitable for a boy or girl. With the advantages of fusible webbing, this project is simple to make, even for beginners.

PLANES 'N' CLOUDS

Beginner

WHAT YOU'LL NEED

- ✈ Sweatshirt
- ✈ Scraps of fabric (we used a striped print, red cotton, white cotton, gold lame, and silver lame)
- ✈ Fabric paints (we used dimensional paints in red, sparkle green, glitter gold, sparkle purple, and pearl white)
- ✈ Double-sided fusible webbing
- ✈ Pencil
- ✈ Iron and ironing board
- ✈ Scissors
- ✈ 2 pressing cloths
- ✈ Shirt board

1. Trace pattern pieces for 3 planes and 4 clouds onto paper side of fusible webbing, grouping together pieces to be cut from same color fabric. (Patterns can be found on page 63.) In the example above, the 3 plane bodies are grouped together because they will be cut from the striped material, the 3 noses and 6 wings are together because they will be cut from the gold lame, the 3 propellers will be cut from the red material, the 3 plane windows will be cut from the silver lame, and the 4 clouds will be cut from the white cotton. (**Note:** If you trace plane pieces so they point to your left, they will point to your right on the finished sweatshirt. Do not trace the dotted lines from the patterns, because they are used just for reference when positioning wings, window, etc., on plane body.)

2. Cut apart pieces in above groupings. In the example above, the 3 plane bodies have been cut apart as one piece of fusible webbing, the clouds have been cut apart as one piece, and so forth.

4. Cut out each plane piece along outside lines. Remove paper from back of each piece. Arrange clouds and body of planes on front of shirt as desired. Tack these pieces in place by pressing point of a hot iron to each for a second or two. Arrange propeller, window, wings, and nose on body of plane and tack in place. Cover arrangement with second pressing cloth. Following manufacturer's instructions, fuse fabric pieces to sweatshirt. Repeat this step, fusing remaining cloud and plane to back of shirt.

3. Cut fabrics into pieces slightly larger than their corresponding webbing groups. Lay a pressing cloth over ironing board. Lay fabrics wrong side up on pressing cloth. With webbing side against wrong side of fabric, place fusible webbing groups over appropriate pieces of fabric (plane bodies piece over striped fabric, nose and wing pieces over gold lame, etc.). Be sure adhesive web does not extend beyond edges of fabric. Cover fusible webbing with second pressing cloth. Following manufacturer's instructions, fuse plane pieces to back of fabrics.

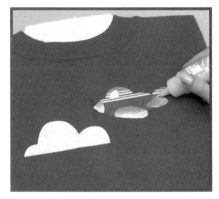

5. Slip sweatshirt over shirt board, placing the side to be painted over the waxed side of the board. Squeezing paints directly from bottle, outline each piece of fabric with fabric paint in color to match. When one side has dried, turn shirt around on board and outline the plane and cloud on other side. (Back of shirt shown above.)

VARIATION

It is difficult to find wearable art designs suitable for boys. Use this fusible webbing technique to create your own designs of trains or automobiles—or, even spaceships and boats. Use the simplified illustrations in coloring books and children's picture books for inspiration.

With this variation of the tie-dye technique so popular in the 1960s, you can make beautiful t-shirts, leggings, and cotton dresses. The secret to a more polished look with tie-dying is to exert more control over the dying process. By updating and refining, this technique will never go out of style.

TIE-DYE BOUQUET

Intermediate

WHAT YOU'LL NEED

- White tunic-styled t-shirt and white cotton leggings
- Thin fabric paint in 4 colors (we used yellow, raspberry, blue, and purple)
- Black fine-point permanent marker
- Rubber bands
- Waxed paper
- Paper towels
- Water in trigger-style sprayer
- Blow dryer
- Iron and ironing board

1. To begin tie-dye process, put one hand inside neck of shirt and poke up a portion of shirt about 3 inches below neckline. Tightly wrap a rubber band around poked-up section so that about ¾ inch of shirt is gathered above the band.

2. Repeat same procedure on both sides of rubber-banded section, about 3 inches to the outside and slightly below this first section. Do 2 more about 3 inches lower and about an inch to each side of center. Insert waxed paper inside of shirt. Be sure it covers entire area to be painted.

3. Work near an electrical outlet. Have blow dryer and spray bottle filled with water on hand. Open all bottles of paint. Squeeze bottle of yellow paint slightly to get paint flowing and then brush onto paper towel. (In general, do not squeeze bottle while brushing on shirt as you may get a bigger burst of paint than you need. Always move bottle of paint over to paper towels when squeezing more paint onto brush.) Brush yellow paint on all poked up sections of shirt above rubber bands. These will be your flower centers.

7. When dry, press shirt on the inside with a warm iron to smooth out wrinkles. Replace waxed paper. Use black fabric marker to lightly sketch in flower stem, flower petals, and details of bow. (Again, you may want to practice this on an old t-shirt first. Use light, quick strokes for best results.)

8. For leggings, gather sections and tie off with rubber bands, as with shirt. This time, however, use a random pattern. There should be a poked-up section every few inches. Insert waxed paper inside legs and seat of leggings. Paint front of legs first. Use brush-top paints as on shirt, coloring centers yellow and selecting flower colors in a random pattern. Try not to put several flowers of the same color next to each other. Immediately mist painted areas with water. Allow to bleed, checking folds as in Step 5. Stop bleeding with blow dryer. Turn leggings over, paint backs of legs, mist, bleed, and dry as before.

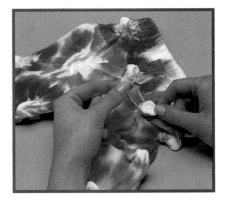

9. Remove all rubber bands from leggings. Keep waxed paper inside and set aside until paint is thoroughly dry. Press leggings on the inside with a warm iron to smooth out wrinkles. Leggings do not require sketched-in flower stems and petals.

4. Brush on other colors below rubber-banded sections in a circle about 1 inch wide. Refer to photo of finished project for recommended color placement.

5. Immediately spray a fine mist of water over painted areas. Check folds near rubber bands to make sure that all areas are bleeding. Add more paint or more water, if necessary. Check progress of bleeding often. Stop bleeding by blowing hot air on paint with a blow dryer until nearly dry and paint is no longer bleeding.

6. Lay shirt flat on work surface, checking to make sure waxed paper covers entire inside of shirt. Add more waxed paper if necessary. Using raspberry paint, make a bow shape below the tie-dye flowers. (You may feel more comfortable practicing on paper towels or an old shirt first.) Mist with water, allow paint to bleed, and then stop bleeding with blow dryer as before. Set shirt aside until completely dry. You may want to remove the rubber bands before painting the bow.

TIP

If you cannot find the brush-top paint in your area, try brushing on fabric dye or diluted fabric paint. Practice on an old t-shirt first to see if you are able to achieve the look you want.

BASEBALL FOREVER

Advanced

Root, root, root for the home team in this cap and shirt decorated with a baseball theme. The easy-to-follow stencil technique shown here makes use of freezer paper, a common household item.

WHAT YOU'LL NEED

- ⚾ White t-shirt and white baseball cap
- ⚾ Dimensional fabric paint in white, black, and red
- ⚾ Soft fabric paint in butterscotch, green, and red
- ⚾ Freezer paper
- ⚾ White paper for tracing pattern
- ⚾ Pencil
- ⚾ Several layers of newspaper or self-healing cutting mat
- ⚾ Craft knife
- ⚾ Iron and ironing board
- ⚾ Shirt board
- ⚾ Palettes
- ⚾ Household sponge cut in 1×1½-inch pieces
- ⚾ Disappearing-ink pen
- ⚾ Red fine-point permanent marker

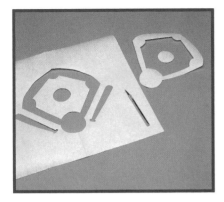

1. Trace pattern onto the edge of white paper. (Pattern can be found on page 64.) Tear off 16-inch piece of freezer paper. Fold freezer paper in half lengthwise, shiny side in. Insert pattern, centering on fold. Trace with pencil and remove. Place freezer paper on layers of newspaper or cutting mat. Keep folded and cut on all lines with a craft knife. Save cut-out pieces of pitcher's mound, infield, and baseline.

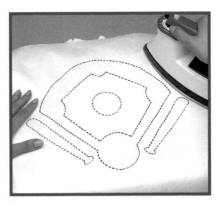

2. Center negative stencil onto shirt shiny side down and iron with a dry iron until freezer paper sticks. Put baseline cut-out on shirt inside of stencil to guide placement of infield cut-out. Place infield cut-out in proper space, remove baseline carefully, and iron infield in place. Insert shirt board, being careful not to pull stencil away from shirt. (Black dotted line has been drawn on stencil for photographic purposes. You do not have to do this at home.)

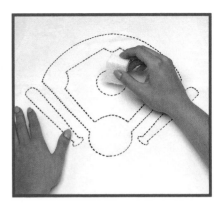

3. Squirt puddle of white dimensional paint onto palette. Moisten piece of household sponge. Be sure to squeeze out all excess water. Use sponge to apply paint to pitcher's mound area of stencil. Make sure paint covers entire area. Check edges of stencil carefully.

4. Pour puddle of butterscotch soft paint onto palette. Use clean piece of sponge to apply paint to baseline area.

5. Remove infield cut-out. Put baseline and pitcher's mound cut-outs in place on shirt directly on top of paint, matching edges as closely as possible. Iron to tack down. (This can be done while paint is still damp. Iron lightly and briefly, or wax may transfer from shirt board to back of shirt. Be careful when applying a new color as stencil edges may pop up.) Pour puddle of green paint onto palette. Use clean sponge to apply to infield area.

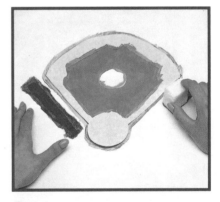

6. Pour puddle of red soft paint onto palette. Use clean sponge to apply to bat areas of stencil. Squirt black dimensional paint onto palette. Use clean sponge to dab about a 1-inch strip of black on handle of bat to represent grip area.

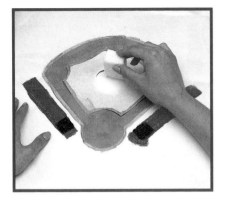

7. Remove pitcher's mound cut-out. Replace infield cut-out. Dab white dimensional paint over previously painted area, using up-and-down motion to give texture to area. Remove and discard all stencils.

8. With disappearing-ink pen draw ¾-inch squares in appropriate areas to represent bases. To make home plate add a triangle to bottom of square (looks like an upside-down house). Beginners may want to draw and cut out paper squares to use as a pattern. Squeezing white dimensional paint directly from the bottle, outline the outside edge of the base and then make thick horizontal lines going back and forth across the base to fill in the area. Complete one base at a time.

9. Using red dimensional paint, draw stitching lines on the pitcher's mound to resemble a baseball. Squeeze paint directly from bottle.

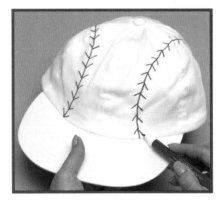

10. To make baseball cap, stuff inside of hat with wads of newspaper to help hold up the crown. Wash hands to remove any newsprint ink. With a disappearing-ink pen, make a mark 2 inches from center on each side of cap, front and back. Connect the front to the back with a curved line. Trace over lines with the red fabric marker.

11. With a tape measure, make a dot with the disappearing-ink pen every ½ inch along lines. Use the dots as a guide to draw slanted lines on each side of long line as shown. Lines on one side of hat slant toward the front, lines on the other side slant toward the back.

TIP

Freezer paper stencils are wonderful for a child's first fabric painting experience. Draw several basic shapes (or trace cookie cutters) on freezer paper and cut out with a craft knife. Iron the negative stencils onto a shirt or an apron, and let the child dab paint inside the stencil with a piece of sponge. Make sure he or she paints all the way to the edges. Your child will get a real kick out of peeling off the freezer paper and seeing the colorful shapes!

Christmas candy canes accent this holiday project for both adults and children. Festive, fun to make, and fabulous to wear, this outfit will rival Santa's red suit for color and charm.

CANDY CANES

WHAT YOU'LL NEED

- Solid color sweatshirt and sweatpants
- 2-4 ozs. white acrylic paint with fine-line applicator
- 108 white 9mm rhinestones
- 108 red 9mm rhinestones
- ⅜ yard ⅝-inch-wide white satin ribbon
- Pencil
- Tracing paper
- 8½×11-inch piece heavy weight card stock
- Dressmaker's pencil or fabric pencil in contrasting color to sweatsuit
- Hole punch
- Needle-nose pliers, or tweezers
- Needle and thread, or fabric glue
- Waxed paper

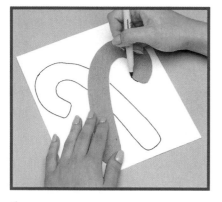

1. Following pattern provided, trace candy cane onto tracing paper and cut along outline. (Pattern can be found on page 55.) Ignore circles along edge of pattern at this time. Position tracing on card stock, outline, and cut from card stock. To make overlapping candy canes for center of shirt, place card-stock cane on paper and trace. Flip over and trace again, intersecting canes at neck. (See photo.) Cut from card stock as one pair.

2. Place candy cane pair into position at center front of sweatshirt about 3 inches from neckline. Outline with dressmaker's pencil or fabric pencil.

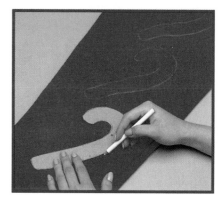

3. Place each single cane into position, spacing evenly along length of one sweatsuit sleeve and one leg. (In our sweatsuit, the candy canes were done on the wearer's left arm and left leg.) Outline all of the candy canes with fabric pencil.

5. Place candy cane tracing over original pattern and mark circles along edge of tracing. Place tracing over card-stock cane and punch holes through tracing and card stock at the marked points.

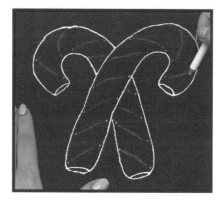

6. Place card-stock cane into position over painted canes. Mark position of holes with fabric pencil. Remove card stock and draw a curved line connecting each pair of holes, as shown. Paint over each connecting line using fine-line applicator.

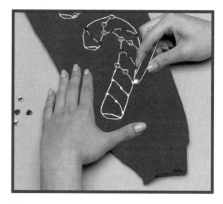

7. Add an extra dab of paint the size of a pea at each end and in the center of connecting lines. Do not allow to dry. Using pliers or tweezers, drop a rhinestone onto each dab of paint, alternating colors at each line. Push rhinestone into paint. Allow to dry thoroughly. It is best to do an entire candy cane at a time, working your way down the sleeve or leg.

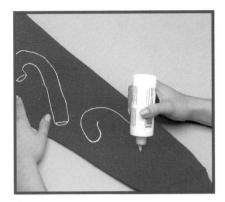

4. Following pencil line, outline all of the candy canes with paint using fine-line applicator. Place waxed paper in sleeve and leg to prevent paint from leaking through fabric. Allow to dry thoroughly.

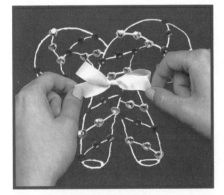

8. Tie ribbon into a bow and stitch or glue to candy cane pair.

TIP

The sweatsuit used here was a size small, adult. The number of candy canes per sleeve and leg may vary according to the size of the sweatsuit. In calculating how many rhinestones you will need for your sweatsuit, figure on 12 of each color for each candy cane.

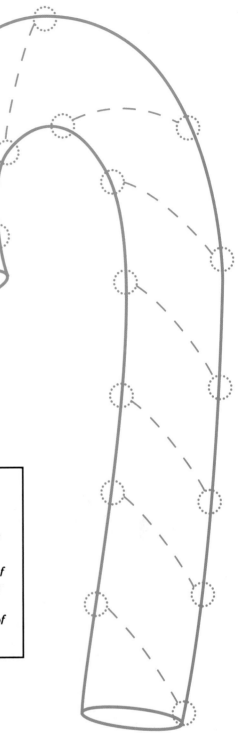

Candy Canes Pattern

TRAVELER'S DENIM JACKET

Advanced

By using photo-transfer medium, you and your child can recycle your family's favorite postcards onto a denim jacket for a one-of-a-kind souvenir of your favorite vacation site.

- 🌴 Denim jacket (stonewashed is best)
- 🌴 ½ yard medium-weight white cotton or cotton blend fabric
- 🌴 Mirror-image color photocopies of about 6 postcards and the map of the state (one of our postcards had several small photos on it that we cut apart and used separately)
- 🌴 Dimensional glitter paint (we used glittering gold platinum)
- 🌴 Round faceted acrylic gemstones to cover buttons or snaps on jacket (ours were 15mm)
- 🌴 Assortment of faceted acrylic gemstones
- 🌴 Assortment of brass charms
- 🌴 Photo-transfer medium
- 🌴 Double-sided fusible webbing
- 🌴 Scissors
- 🌴 Waxed paper
- 🌴 1-inch sponge brush
- 🌴 Rolling pin
- 🌴 Iron and ironing board
- 🌴 Pressing cloth
- 🌴 Disappearing-ink pen
- 🌴 Washable glue
- 🌴 Palette
- 🌴 Industrial strength adhesive
- 🌴 Toothpicks
- 🌴 Pliers

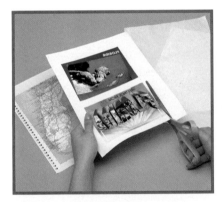

1. Tentatively plan the placement of postcards and map on your jacket. Do this before you have your copies made so you know what you will need. After photocopying your postcards and map, trim white edges from postcard photocopies as shown. If you included a postcard with several photos on it that you want to use individually, cut them apart. Do not trim photocopy of state map. Cut white fabric into 4 or 5 rectangles about 9×12 inches as shown. These will be easier to work with than a single strip of fabric. Place each piece of white fabric on a sheet of waxed paper.

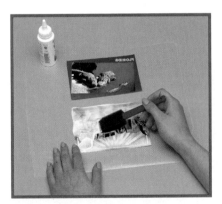

2. Lay photocopies, including map, face up on separate sheets of waxed paper. Working on a copy at a time, apply a thick layer of transfer medium with your finger or a sponge brush. Be sure all edges and corners have been covered.

TIP

When selecting charms, consider the geography and character of the state you've chosen. Sailboats and seashells work well for an ocean-side state, but snowflakes would be good for the north, while cowboy boots may work well for a western state.

3. Place each copy face down on white fabric. Smooth with fingers and rolling pin, being sure to remove any air bubbles. If any transfer medium is pressed out of sides, wipe it up immediately. Leave about an inch of fabric border around all copies. Dry flat for 24 hours. After 24 hours, remove fabric from waxed paper and heat-set both sides of transfers for 30 seconds using a pressing cloth and a dry iron on a wool setting. Let cool.

4. Soak transfers in water for 30-60 minutes. Remove from water. Squeeze excess water from fabric as much as possible, but do not wring transfer area. Lay fabric on a clean, flat surface. Using your fingers, gently rub off paper backing. Work from the center of the transfer to the outside edges. When you have removed the first layer of paper, return fabric to water to soak for another 15 minutes. Remove from water, repeating process until all paper particles have been removed. Be especially careful when rubbing edges so as not to tear the transfer. Let fabric dry flat. (Transfers may appear cloudy. They will become more defined when washable glue is applied later, but they will never be as clear as the original.)

5. Cut a rectangle of fusible webbing slightly smaller than each piece of fabric. When all paper particles have been removed and fabric is dry, follow manufacturer's instructions and fuse webbing to back of all fabric pieces.

9. When glue is dry, outline cards and map with dimensional glitter paint. Be sure to keep tip of bottle on fabric. Do the front of jacket, then, when paint is dry, turn over and do the back.

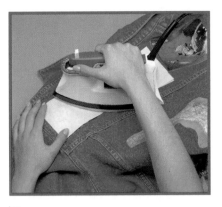

6. Using a disappearing-ink pen, draw a line just outside the state's borders on the map. Cut on the line. Cut postcard from fabric pieces along edges of cards.

7. Remove paper backing from adhesive on the back of transfers. On a hard surface (not a padded ironing board cover), arrange photo transfers of map and postcards as desired on jacket. Cover transfers with pieces of paper backing from iron-on adhesive, shiny side down to protect your iron and your transfer. Follow manufacturer's instructions for fusing. Iron on all transfers, front and back.

8. Pour a puddle of washable glue onto palette and use sponge brush to apply a thin, even coat to transfers on front of jacket. If some of the transfer edges are popping up, spread a small amount of glue underneath. When front is dry, repeat for the transfers on the back.

10. After paint dries, arrange acrylic gemstones in desired spots on back of jacket. We used a star on the state capital, a heart on our favorite city, and various sizes and colors of round stones on different cities throughout the state. We used 15mm round stones and plastic dogwood leaves to represent oranges, and we placed 15mm stones on the back buttons. Use pliers to remove holes from brass charms, if desired. Arrange charms on back of jacket.

11. Lift up one gem or charm at a time and use a toothpick to apply industrial strength glue to backs. Work in a well ventilated area to avoid inhaling fumes from glue. Do not allow children around this type of glue. To glue round gems to metal buttons, use toothpick to spread a layer of glue on the back of gem and on the top of the metal button. Allow each to dry for about 10 minutes before pressing together.

12. Turn jacket over and arrange gems and charms on the front. Glue charms and gems on jacket and buttons as directed in Step 11.

Making a Splash!

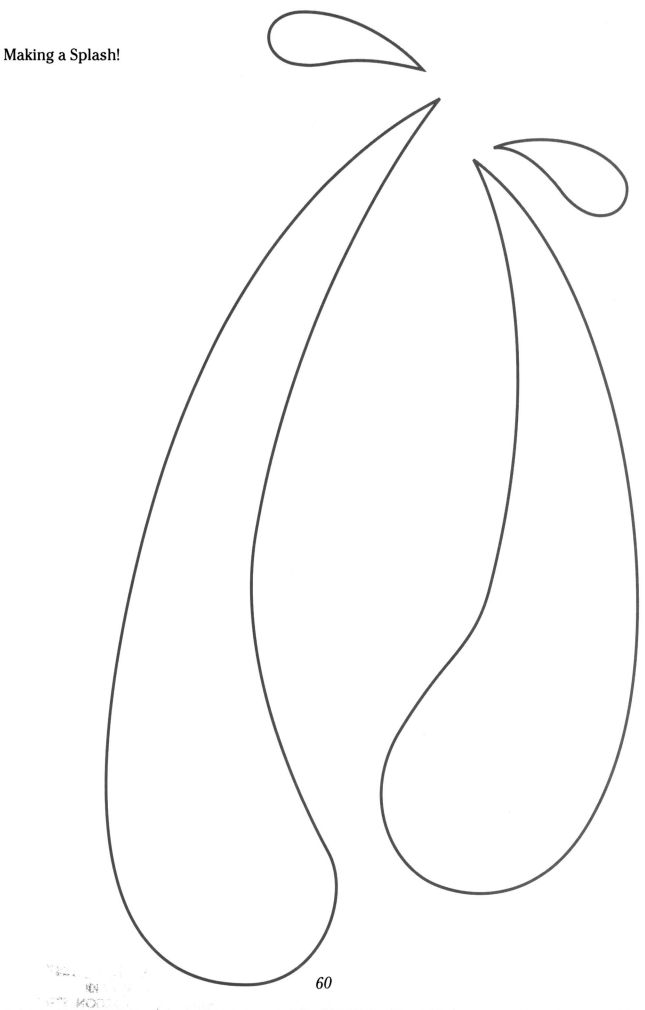

(Pattern bottom)

Fun at the Beach

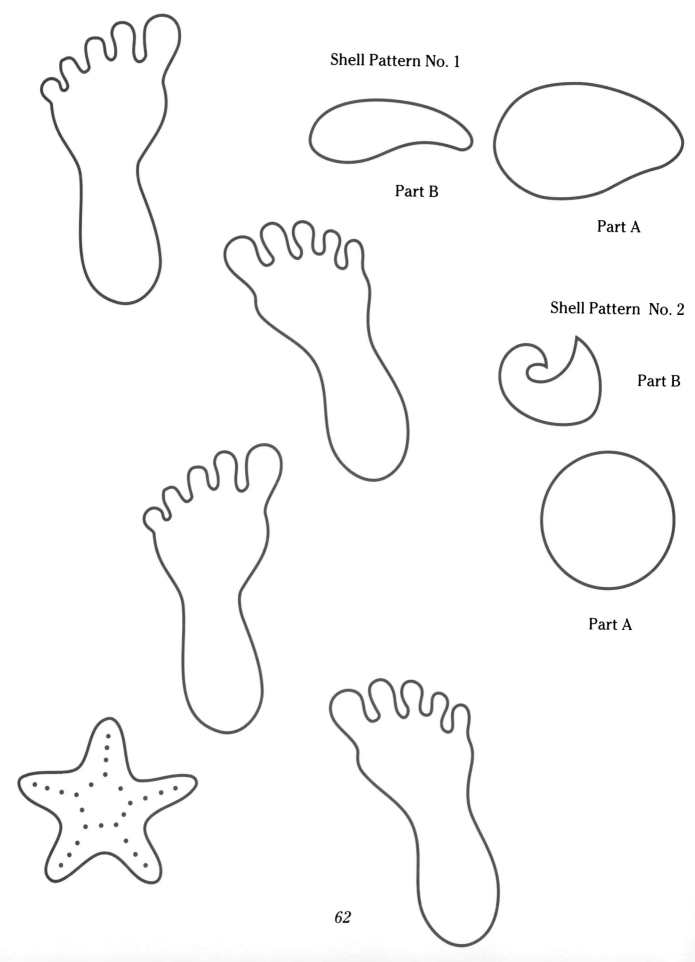

Shell Pattern No. 1

Part B

Part A

Shell Pattern No. 2

Part B

Part A

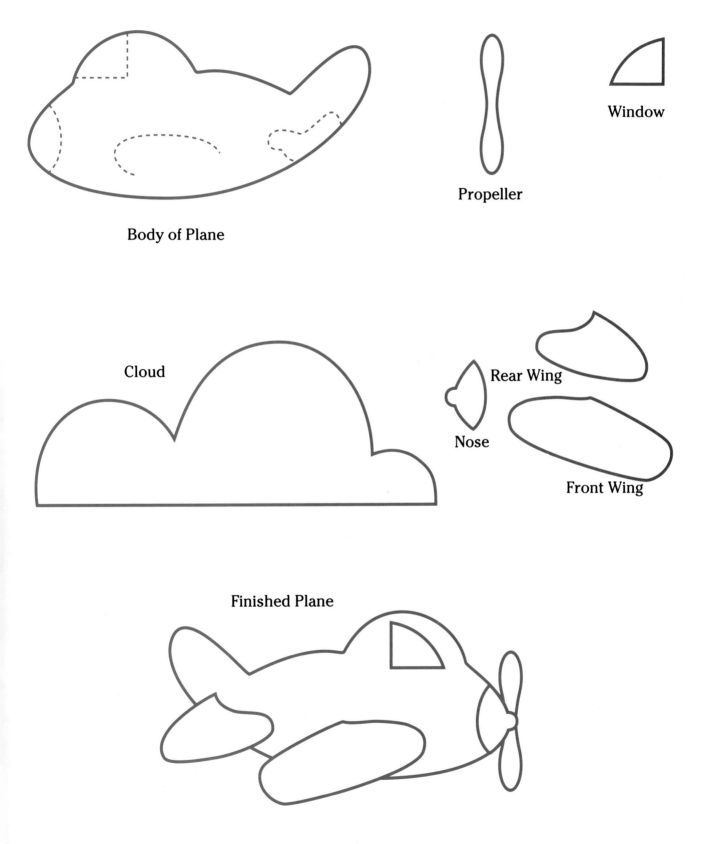

Body of Plane

Propeller

Window

Cloud

Rear Wing

Nose

Front Wing

Finished Plane

Baseball Forever

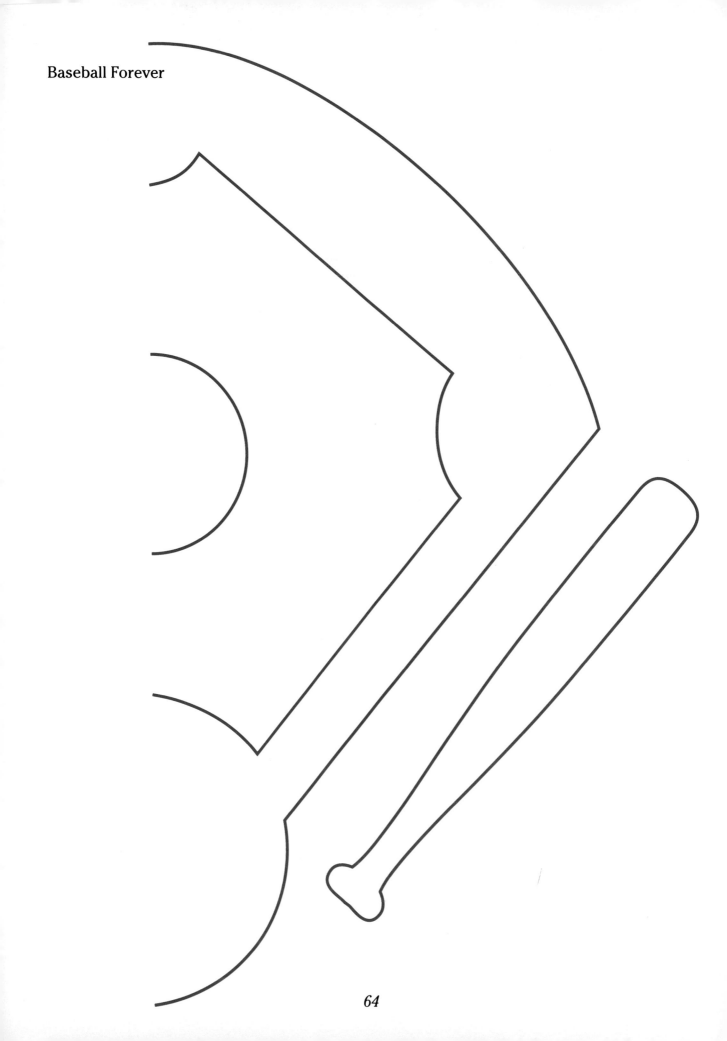